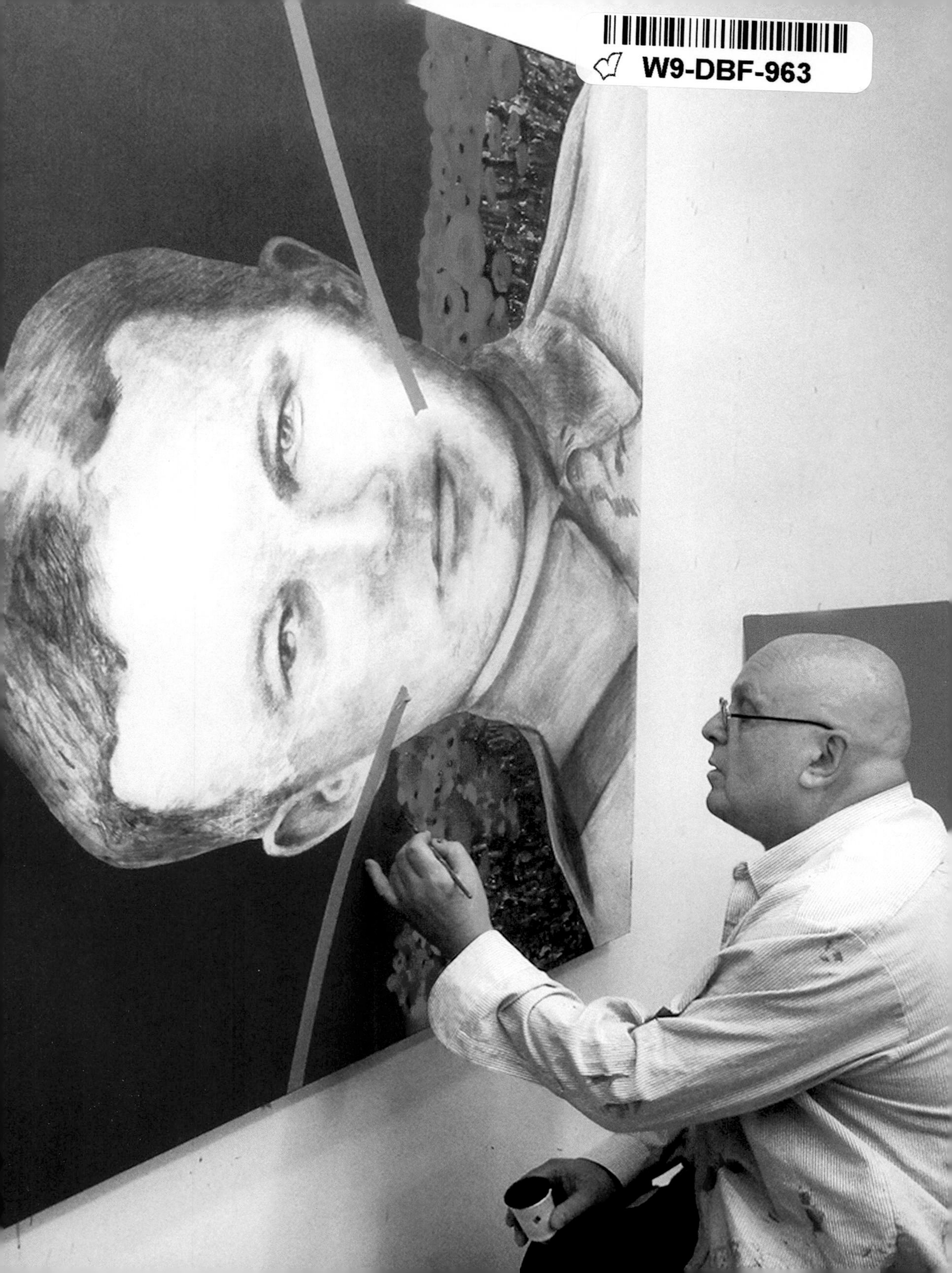

SO
I
GUESS
THAT'S
IT
THEN

Published in conjunction with the exhibition
Charles Pachter: Lest We Forget
June 19, 2014

Lest We Forget: Paintings by Charles Pachter Commemorating the First World War

Office of the Lieutenant Governor of Ontario
Queen's Park, Toronto, Ontario, Canada M7A 1A1
www.lgontario.ca

ISBN 978-1-4606-4368-6 (Print)   ISBN 978-1-4606-4369-3 (PDF)
Ce livre est aussi disponible en français

Photographs: p. 1 courtesy of C. Pachter; p. 2–3 James Bowers; p. 11 Debi Perna; p. 15 eVeritas; p. 19 Gordon Kogawa; p. 23 courtesy of I. Abuelaish; p. 27 Mark Burnett (portrait), Associated Press (1972 photo); p. 31 courtesy of J. L. Granatstein; p. 37 Canadian Press (Nichola Goddard), courtesy of S. Goddard (portrait); p. 41 Peter Bregg; p. 47 Norman Wong; p. 51 courtesy of M. MacMillan; p. 55 Keith Beaty, Toronto Star; p. 59 courtesy of Office of Jean Chrétien; p. 60 courtesy of C. Pachter.

Design: Debi Perna, PS Design
Printed in Canada by C.J. Graphics Inc.

The Office of the Lieutenant Governor is grateful for the support of the Archives of Ontario.

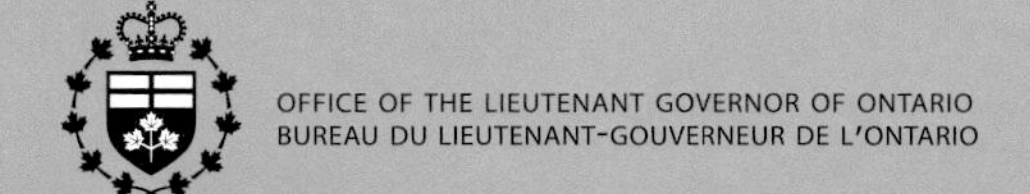

LEST WE FORGET

PAINTINGS BY CHARLES PACHTER COMMEMORATING THE FIRST WORLD WAR

PRESENTED BY THE OFFICE OF
THE LIEUTENANT GOVERNOR OF ONTARIO

Essays by

Izzeldin Abuelaish
Joseph Boyden
Jean Chrétien
Roméo A. Dallaire
John de Chastelain
Mellissa Fung
Sally Goddard
J. L. Granatstein
Joy Kogawa
Margaret MacMillan
Charles Pachter
Kim Phuc Phan Thi

Night, The Canvas House I

Symbolic depictions of the canvas tent as temporary shelter from the elements.

Acrylic on canvas, 126 x 105 cm

The Hon. David C. Onley

FOREWORD

The twentieth century saw Canadians volunteer to fight in the devastating conflicts of the First and Second World Wars and Korea. Over 115,000 of them gave their lives, an experience that has profoundly shaped our nation's collective memory.

I have always been aware of the attributes of war, and increasingly so during my term as Lieutenant Governor.

My great uncle is buried in France, having died at the Somme in 1916. My father and father-in-law both served in the Royal Canadian Air Force in World War II. Several of my aides-de-camp have served in Afghanistan and I have had the sad honour of participating in Silver Cross presentations for Ontario soldiers killed in that conflict.

Although it has been over two centuries since a Lieutenant Governor of Ontario last commanded troops in battle, this office has always maintained close ties with our military. During times of war, Lieutenant Governors have personified the Crown's unifying force and have inspired camaraderie and the determination to succeed. During peacetime, they have brought us together in remembrance and tribute of those who paid the ultimate sacrifice.

Many of my predecessors who served in the First and Second World Wars could readily relate to this role. Lieutenant Governors such as Henry Cockshutt, Herbert Bruce, John Keiller MacKay, W. Ross MacDonald, John Black Aird, and Lincoln Alexander all knew the realities of war. Their collective experiences—as doctors, soldiers, sailors, airmen and officers—were firsthand and personal and helped ensure that Ontarians would never lose sight of the impact of war on our society.

On the occasion of the centenary of the First World War, the Office of the Lieutenant Governor is hosting *Lest We Forget*, an exhibition of paintings by Charles Pachter, one of Canada's leading contemporary artists.

Accompanying the exhibition is a collection of essays by a distinguished and diverse group of Canadians who reflect on the question "What Have We Learned From War?"

Their responses illustrate the complex and conflicting nature of war, its capacity to elicit our most destructive instincts, as well as our greatest examples of courage, heroism and camaraderie.

I thank them for their contributions and salute all who have served.

Tank Top

Surrealist composition that came to me in a dream of a nurse wearing a tank as a hat—this was the first war to employ the tank, a formidable new weapon of destruction and defence.

Inkjet on canvas, 100 x 120 cm

Charles Pachter

THOUGHTS ON THE WAR TO END ALL WARS

Where have all the soldiers gone?
Gone to graveyards, everyone
Oh, when will they ever learn? When will they ever learn?

— Pete Seeger, *Where Have All The Flowers Gone?*

Recently, I created a series of paintings examining the War of 1812 between the young United States and Britain's North American colonies that resulted in the birth of a new Canadian identity.

A century later came the First World War. And a century after that, I was approached by the Office of the Lieutenant Governor of Ontario to consider painting a series about this "war to end all wars" that defined our emerging colonial nation with even more profound and tragic consequences.

If this was Canada's coming of age, its profound rite of passage, I needed to know why fighting for the British Empire was seen to be such an act of courage and loyalty, why young men from across the vast reaches of our sparsely populated country of just eight million people left for the battlefields of Germany, France and Belgium to be wounded, slaughtered and, if they survived, traumatized for life.

For months, I pored over letters written by young soldiers from the trenches, diaries of courageous nurses, and dour military reports of the appalling number of casualties among Canada's young soldiers.

My thoughts turned to a painting I remembered from childhood by Group of Seven war artist Frederick Varley titled *FOR WHAT?* which depicts a grisly pile of mutilated corpses in a cart sitting in a filthy quagmire, awaiting hasty burial.

The more I read, the more I pondered war as the low point of human existence. How different were we, are we, from the apes? How have we evolved, if at all? Is killing for territory and dominance an inevitable characteristic of human behaviour?

After much sifting of ideas, I chose not to depict the violence and savagery of the battlefields, the exploding shells, the gunfire, the rotting corpses, and the agony of the wounded and dying.

Instead, I chose a path of meditation on War as Metaphor.

Wordsworth's phrase, "Emotion recollected in tranquility", often came to my mind. One hundred years later, could I evoke this war as a metaphor for human frailty? Could I transform misery and suffering into something powerful, poetic, metaphysical?

An excerpt from John McCrae's celebrated poem *In Flanders Fields* kick-started my subconscious:

We are the Dead. Short days ago
We lived, felt dawn, saw sunset glow,
Loved and were loved, and now we lie
In Flanders fields.

My challenge was to get up close and personal with The Warrior—to put myself in his boots, to get my head inside his brain, to feel what one lone soldier felt confronting his rage, his fear, his mortality.

And I also wondered how the stoic nurses, the healers, survived deprivation, discomfort, shock. How they must have needed and clung to each other for friendship and moral support.

I tried to imagine myself in the position of a half-naked soldier contemplating the possibility of his demise.

"Death be not proud," wrote John Donne nearly 400 years ago.

And Shakespeare's Hamlet, "For in that sleep of death what dreams may come."

The same themes kept haunting me:

Trench
Gas Mask
Tank
Tent
Nurse
Warplane
Battleship

I refer to my painting style as *Reductionist Symbolism*, whereby I tried to reduce an idea to its essence. I have attempted a Zen-like examination of pure form, inspired and motivated by the above themes. I have endeavoured to meld the Left and Right sides of the brain (analytic and emotional) to come together to invite contemplation of the eternal questions based on the subject painted:

What is War, What is Peace
What is Life, What is Death
What is Love, What is Hate
What is Existence, What is Transcendence
What is Deliverance

And finally,
What is Hope, What is Joy

Charles Pachter, OC is a painter, printmaker, sculptor, designer, historian, and lecturer. His work has been exhibited at the Art Gallery of Ontario, the Royal Ontario Museum, and the McMichael Gallery. He is represented in public and private collections throughout Canada and internationally. He holds honorary doctorates from Brock University, OCAD University, and the University of Toronto, where he is a Senior Fellow at Massey College.

Gasp

The first war to use gas masks to avoid being poisoned. Even the animals wore them. The terrified look in the horse's eye says it all.

Acrylic and pastel on canvas, 122 x 183 cm

Gen. John de Chastelain (retd)

WHAT HAVE WE LEARNED FROM WAR? CANADA 1914 – 2014

One hundred years ago, with a population of seven and a quarter million citizens, Canada fought a four-year war in Europe in which more than 60,000 of its soldiers were killed and approximately 153,000 wounded. This year Canada, with a population of more than thirty-five million, after fighting in five more wars and participating in numerous others, ends its role in the Afghanistan war, in which 158 Canadians soldiers were killed and nearly two thousand were casualties. Those numbers say much about how the state of both the world and of war has changed during that hundred year period, as it does about how Canada and its involvement in war has changed also. So what have we learned about war in that time?

On the negative side we've learned yet again that modern war is enormously costly and brings death and injury to participants and civilians alike, and massive ruin to infrastructure. We've learned that nuclear weapons of war, if used in a major conflict, have the capacity to end civilisation as we know it, but we have not yet found the means to destroy or outlaw them effectively. Instead, we've learned to live with their existence, and to accept that the concept of mutually assured destruction (MAD) can act as a deterrent against nuclear adventurism. And for the past seventy-eight years it has done so.

We've learned too that there is a positive side to war, even as we seek to ensure it does not happen. Sometimes nationhood comes at the price of war, and a nation's continued existence can demand a willingness to fight to defend it. Prior to becoming a nation 147 years ago, Canada was the scene of frequent conflict involving British, French, American and First Nations combatants, and only recently, Canada commemorated the bicentenary of a war fought on Canadian soil between British and American forces.

Indeed, Canada's move to nationhood at Charlottetown in 1867 was accelerated over fears caused by Fenian raids launched from America into Ontario and New Brunswick the year before. Thirty years later, Canada provided more than seven thousand soldiers to fight alongside Britain in South Africa, and in 1914, when Britain declared war on Germany, Canada, under the terms of its then Dominion status, was automatically at war too.

Canada's performance in World War I enhanced its move to full independence through the professionalism of its fighting forces in the major battles, as it did when Sir Arthur Currie's 1st Canadian Corps captured Vimy Ridge in 1917 after allied attempts failed.

In 1939, now politically autonomous after the 1931 *Statute of Westminster*, Canada joined Britain in declaring war on Germany at its own volition, not because Canada was threatened at home, but because of its belief in the need to counter the threat of fascism, following Germany's invasion of Czechoslovakia and Poland.

The value to its allies of Canada's participation in that war was evident not only in the quality of its one million fighting men and women who took part, but also in the supply of vast amounts of *matériel* and arms shipped to Russia and Britain via the North Atlantic. Also significant was the British Commonwealth Air Training Plan, in which Canada trained over 180,000 air crew and 80,000 ground crew for the allies. That Canada ended the war with the third largest surface Navy in the world and the fourth largest Air Force demonstrated its will to play a full role as an ally in this eminently just war.

The fact that nuclear weapons were used to end the Pacific war in 1945 increased the possibility that war could be waged against Canadians at home. Heretofore isolated from conflict in Europe, Canada's homeland was now threatened by the deployment of intercontinental and submarine-launched ballistic missiles. To defend such a geographically vast country, with three oceans and a small population, Canada could only hope to do so through alliance with other countries. Thus, Canada joined the United States and Western European nations in the North Atlantic Treaty Organization (NATO), and the United States in the North American Air Defence Command (NORAD). It also pledged to provide troops to the newly formed United Nations Organization, should that become necessary.

Countering invasion elsewhere was the reason Canada fought in the United Nations operations in Korea in 1950, and in Iraq forty years later, but it was also why Canada stationed land and air forces in West Germany in 1951 under NATO command, when the presence of Soviet troops in East Germany and Eastern Europe was seen as a threat. That the Cold War in Europe ended peacefully, despite the NATO – Warsaw Pact confrontation there, justified the belief that a demonstrated willingness to engage in war to defend a cause was a significant way to help prevent it.

At the beginning of the Cold War, and after the 1956 invasion of Egypt by Britain, France and Israel, Canadian Lester Pearson's initiative to have a United Nations Emergency Force intervene whilst peacemakers sought to negotiate a settlement launched a new era for Canada in peacekeeping. The idea of changing Canada's role to predominantly peacekeeping was attractive to Canadians who liked to think of their country as an "honest broker", and to politicians who saw in it the possibility of avoiding the major expenditures needed to man and equip forces for a conventional land,

General John de Chastelain, CH, OC, CMM, CD is a retired Canadian soldier and diplomat. He served twice as Canadian Chief of the Defence Staff, and was head of the International Commission on Decommissioning in Northern Ireland (1997 – 2011).

sea and air war abroad. That concept notwithstanding, Canada continued to prepare for possible war in Europe and kept its forces stationed there and in the North Atlantic until the Cold War ended in 1989.

In recent years, international terrorism has added to dangers faced by Canadians at home. While the concept of another major land, sea and air war involving millions, as in 1914 and 1939, seems unlikely to recur, the war on terrorism has taken on a new urgency following terrorist attacks against the United States, Spain and Britain at the beginning of this century.

Given its involvement in the war in Afghanistan, Canada has been targeted by imported and home-grown would-be jihadists, and while attempts to carry out terrorist attacks on Canadian soil have been thwarted so far, continued vigilance and an enhanced intelligence and security establishment remains necessary to counteract the threat.

Terrorist threats aside, Canada's attitude to war continues to be to prevent it if possible, but to engage in it alongside allies if that becomes necessary. That, essentially, is what Canada has learned from engagement in the wars of the past century. It is why Canada's defence policy continues to be defined in its three main defence objectives: the defence of Canada itself; the defence of North America in co-operation with the United States; and contributing to international security. Each objective continues to include the possibility of going to war, and today, as Canada begins the second century following its 1914 experience, that seems unlikely to change.

The Healers

Angels of mercy, dauntless nurses from all over Canada, who tended the wounds of dying soldiers brought in from the battlefields.

Acrylic and pastel on canvas, 122 x 198 cm

Joy Kogawa

WORK IN PROGRESS: GENTLY TO NAGASAKI

Chapter Two

For well over a decade, *Gently to Nagasaki* was a title without a book, tenacious and puzzling, a peg on the bathroom door with no garment hanging from it. In the past it was the other way around. Books were finished, handed over, and still—no title.

Why did I have this title? *Gently to Nagasaki*?

In the late 1970s, I finished a draft of a semi-autobiographical novel. The book had no title, and in the end, was given a title I had not thought up: *Obasan*.

For the most part, what happened to the fictional family in the novel was what happened to mine. We Canadians of Japanese ancestry found ourselves suddenly enemies of our country, because Canada was at war with Japan. We were "evacuated" in 1942 to the mountains of interior British Columbia. None of us returned to our homes, mine being in Vancouver.

The family in my novel ended up after the war on the Prairies, as did we. But throughout the story was a mystery. The young mother had gone to Japan before the war and disappeared there. This was entirely fictional. My real mother never left.

"What happened to the mother?" asked Louise Dennys, of Lester & Orpen Dennys, the publisher who finally accepted the book.

"I don't know. I think she vanished," I said. "Isn't life like that? People disappear. Isn't that what happens in real life?"

"The reader has to know, Joy. You need to go back and revisit the question," she said.

I took the book back into myself, and searched for the answer. Where did the mother go? The answer to the mystery arrived, and inserted itself as a clue.

August 9.

That is the day the atom bomb was dropped on Nagasaki. That is where the missing young mother in *Obasan* was in 1945. That is where I, as the author, placed her. But where that answer to the mystery of my creation came from, I have no idea. It was not a city about which I knew anything, except that it had been bombed.

Now, decades later, re-examining the themes in my work, incubating new thoughts and feelings, and going Gently, to Nagasaki, I have come to understand that now, there is a specific lesson I am to learn. The lesson is this: every enemy is a beloved friend.

That lesson, that treasure, is in the midst of the devastation known as Nagasaki.

What has struck me with some fascination was the significance for Christians of August 6 and August 9, the two dates the atom bombs fell on Japan. The first, Hiroshima Day, is called the Day of Transfiguration in some Christian calendars. On that day, Jesus is said to have gone up a mountain with his three closest disciples, Peter, James and John. While the three looked up in fear, Elijah and Moses, the prophet and the law-giver, appeared on either side of Jesus, whose form had become "exceeding white". Mark 9:3. …And his garments became glistering, exceeding white…. The man who healed the sick, restored the sight of the blind and made the deaf to hear, the man from Galilee, was "transfigured." The light within him was, for a moment, made visible on the outside.

So it was, that on the day commemorating Christ's transfiguration, the city and citizens of Hiroshima were obliterated.

A little boy looked up and saw a white parachute against the sky. "Look at the parachute!" he cried just before a bright glistering light of death like no other flashed upon the world and changed us forever.

My brother, a retired Episcopalian priest in Seattle, told me that the word "transfiguration" (in Japanese *hen-yo-bo*) also meant "disfiguration." The Day of Transfiguration became then, on August 6, 1945, the Day of Disfiguration. This one word with two meanings and the two events on the same day merged in my mind. The transfigured one was disfigured. The disfigured one was transfigured.

For centuries, until about forty years ago, the story of the transfiguration was read on a Sunday that was followed three days later by Ash Wednesday, a day of fasting and penitence. The Day of Trans/Disfiguration in 1945 was followed, three days later, by an unparalleled day of ashes. The second bomb fell on August 9 with pinpoint precision, directly over the pre-eminent spot of Christianity in all of East Asia.

If ever the Christian West had friends in Japan, it was there, in a valley between mountains. That sacred place, the Urakami neighbourhood in Nagasaki, was home to Japan's Hidden Christians, a people who had survived centuries of the most grotesque tortures and martyrdoms. The surviving remnant had come home from exile at last, to safety, to their neighbourhood and to the finally tolerated practice of their faith. There they worked in the fields as farmers and re-built their lives. The Christians that Japan failed to annihilate after centuries of unimaginable cruelty, the Christian West managed to do in an instant.

It has been said what makes humans unique is not that we use tools—other animals

Joy Kogawa, CM, OBC is a Canadian poet and novelist of Japanese descent. She was sent with her family to the internment camp for Japanese Canadians at Slocan, British Columbia, during World War II. She works to educate Canadians about the history of the internment camps, and was active in the fight for government redress. This piece is an excerpt from a work-in-progress entitled *Gently to Nagasaki*, and has been adapted for this project.

do that, nor that we have language—that too is an attribute of other animals, but that we are creatures who seek meaning. For many people, particularly following the Holocaust in Europe, the search for meaning is heinous. The answer to the question of meaning is that there is no meaning.

But I cannot accept meaninglessness as an answer to Nagasaki. For me, that incomprehensible event on August 9, 1945, the immolation by the Christian West of its Christian family in Asia, means that a certain truth has been made starkly visible. It provides the moment for recognizing what lies behind the words of Jesus the Christ. At Nagasaki, the impossible proscription "Love your enemy" is transformed into a description, "You love your enemy". We no longer have to love the enemy. All we have to do is to realize that we already do love them without knowing that we do.

The task for me then, the arduous but happy task, is to recognize this. For the rest of my life, what is required is to discover the ways in which this is true. If I move by thought or word or deed, to defeat or deface an enemy, I am acting to harm a beloved friend, one who is of greatest value and to whom I owe deep loyalty.

The Goddess of Mercy is there in Japan the beautiful, Japan the terrible, Japan the country of my ancestors. Although I fail Her lessons again and again, She teaches me patiently that the enemy is not an enemy. It is Her presence I attend as She leads the way gently, to the place where the sacred children of the Hidden Christians died begging for water.

Water, my Goddess.

Omizu kudasai!

Lament

Post Traumatic Stress Disorder, common to many soldiers haunted for life by the ghastly events of battle.

Acrylic and pastel on canvas, 102 x 66 cm

Dr. Izzeldin Abuelaish

INTERACTING WITH WAR BEYOND THE SCREEN

If ever it may happen in the future, today war cannot be halted. Tragically, the ravages of war are not limited to the battlefield; the combatants are not limited to soldiers; and the damage extends into every facet of society, including family, the economy, healthcare, education, governance, and infrastructure, for generations. And, as Eleanor Roosevelt said: "No one won the last war and no one will win the next war." War is the ultimate ugliness that rains down on us from the clouds of prejudice, greed, and hatred. We are all born equal, yet are treated differently, based on nothing but the law of the jungle. War starts because of differences of race, religion, skin colour, and territoriality.

War in the human world is even worse than the law of the jungle. Animals kill to survive and to defend themselves; humans kill based on venality. War coats everything with death. Although soldiers are considered to be the main casualties of war, it is often civilians who make up the vast majority of deaths. In fact, a large proportion of casualties are women and children. While soldiers are supposedly ready to giving up their lives for the sake of their country, civilian populations do not sign up for danger. Although combat-related causalities have declined, civilian causalities have increased.

Even though we see gore, blood, poverty, and destitution on television, these images are merely a fraction of the reality of war on the ground.

The fear, the tears, the state of limbo, and the loneliness of the soul during times of war are unfathomable. Children are left to pick up the shards of their mental health, having seen their own bodies disfigured, and their loved ones' limbs blown up. Hundreds of thousands die before their time. They die without having contributed a fraction of what they're capable of giving to the world.

War is genocide, torture, cruelty, propaganda, dishonesty, and the enslavement of humanity. Portrayed on television as if it were a Hollywood thriller, war is presented as a live documentary about a distant topic. Instead of summoning our efforts to document the ugliness of war, showing every detail as if it were only scientific research, we must work extremely hard to try and prevent it. Caused by ignorance and prejudice, war can be prevented through education. By 2020, the World Health Organization and the World Bank predict that war will be the eighth leading cause of disability and death. Speaking up against war should be our number-one priority.

If we acknowledge that war directly affects all of us, and is not just a distant event on television, we will help bring humanity closer. We have succeeded in containing HIV/AIDS, fighting cancer, and have even reached the moon. Replacing ignorance with positive action should also be possible. Teaching ourselves that all humans are born equal, teaching our children to respect others regardless of their race, religion, sex, or age this is the legacy we must leave. We need to work together to prevent wars and conflict in their infancy, rather than wage war. Our children will eventually grow up and lead the world, hopefully rendering it more peaceful. For if a good seed is planted in them, this seed will grow into a good plant.

And that, in the end, is the best kind of victory. Peace is the ultimate prize, not more wealth, territory, or power.

Peace is freedom. It is the pleasure of knowing that we and our children matter no more and no less than others and their children do. Peace is living in health and in recognition of others' right to live differently while enjoying the freedom to live as we please. We must teach our children to resolve inevitable disputes through harmonious communication because, according to Margaret Atwood, "war is what happens when language fails". Peace is knowing that our children will grow up in a safe and secure world, able to develop into healthy adults who bring happiness to those around them. In the end, I believe that life is what we make it. It has always been that way. We put our effort into making it matter and it rewards us in kind. And so we must declare that our common enemy is war and hatred, not each other.

And lest we listen only to people of peace, let us also heed no less a man of war than Dwight D. Eisenhower, a five-star general in the United States Army and Supreme Commander of the Allied Forces in Europe during World War II, who said:

> *"Every gun that is made, every warship launched, every rocket fired signifies in the final sense, a theft from those who hunger and are not fed, those who are cold and are not clothed. This world in arms is not spending money alone. It is spending the sweat of its laborers, the genius of its scientists, and the hopes of its children. This is not a way of life at all in any true sense."*

Dr. Izzeldin Abuelaish, OOnt is a Palestinian medical doctor and author living in Toronto. He founded the *Daughters for Life Foundation* in memory of three of his daughters and a niece, who were killed during the Gaza War. He wrote the acclaimed memoir *I Shall Not Hate* and is currently an associate professor of global health at the University of Toronto.

I believe that by speaking out against war we will take steps toward the path of peace. Although it is much harder to build and teach than to destroy, the rewards of constructing peace are much richer and more durable and satisfying. It's my solid belief that safeguarding the dignity, safety, and well-being of human beings in any conflict exceeds any other consideration.

Building close ties between people is one of the most effective ways of preventing conflict over the long term. These ties should be built on equality, respect, and freedom. It is to these people—the hundreds of thousands of men, women, and children who crave a normal, peaceful, and economically stable life—that the international community must devote greater attention. It is they who collectively represent the best chance for peace, and yet, are ironically compelled to bear the brunt of its perennial absence.

In order to succeed, we must push the limit beyond the edge of what is possible today. We must smash barriers and exceed the limits of both the visible and invisible. We must learn to see beyond what is available today, drawing upon wisdom and insight in order to push our humanity forward from the rubble of its own self-destruction.

Night, The Canvas House II

Symbolic depictions of the canvas tent as temporary shelter from the elements.

Acrylic on canvas, 91 x 183 cm

Kim Phuc Phan Thi

WHAT HAVE WE LEARNED FROM WAR?

Without faith, we are hopeless. Without hope, we are lost. For a time I felt lost, and betrayed by the government that won the Vietnam War. My conversion to Christianity filled me with the grace and courage I needed to survive my scars, and the scars of my people. This would be my destiny.

As a little child, I had no cares. My family lived in a large house, we had land, and we were rich, as far as village life went. I remember the tall trees, and climbing them to reach big, juicy guavas. I remember when it rained and how good it felt. We children had to make our own fun, and would run and play, sliding in the water after a rainfall. Everything seemed perfect.

As a little child, I didn't know what was going on in the larger world, but I did know my parents were always scared. Sometimes my father would go to the town to sleep overnight. I'd ask my mother "Where is father?" and she would tell us, but never give us the reason why he left. It is only later we found out he had to leave, or else he might be taken away by the Viet Cong. There were two doors in our house, and when people came, they would knock differently. The front door was a friendly knock, but the back door knock would be the Viet Cong. My mother owned a restaurant in the village, and at night she would walk down the road, holding a torch to light her way, and pass severed heads on the road. If you didn't do what the Viet Cong said, you were in trouble. My parents did their best to protect us.

The day the bombs dropped, everything changed. In an instant, my happy life was gone. The napalm seared me, and I was not expected to survive. I stayed in the hospital in Saigon for 14 months, and I had 17 operations. The doctors and nurses cared for me compassionately, and they inspired me. I thought, when I got home, I would like to study, to be a doctor. They helped me live.

The Communists had other plans, and used me as a propaganda tool. My studies were cut short by the local government and the officials offered me a job of manual work. I knew that I would have to work with my mind, and work lightly, rather than do hard physical work, because I was not able. When they took away my studies, they took away my dreams, and I felt like they took away my life.

I felt isolated. I was 18 years old and I had no one to talk to. I began to hate my life and to hate "normal" people. I felt ugly and disfigured and thought that no one would ever want me. In 1982 I wanted to give up. The government controlled us, and I didn't want to be controlled any longer, I didn't want my mind to be controlled. I remember being on a street corner in Saigon contemplating suicide, by jumping into traffic.

At this time, on my break from work, I would go to the library and read. I only had an hour, and I pored over religious books, seeking, always seeking. The religion I grew up with, Cao Dai, didn't make sense to me anymore. Then I came across the Bible, and started to read the New Testament. Very slowly, I became open to love. I think of John 14:6. *"I am the way, and the truth, and the life; no one comes to the Father but through Me."* That became my way, and I converted to Christianity.

When President Nixon doubted the authenticity of the photograph taken by Nick Ut, it surprised me. The Associated Press ran the photo; how could it not be true? My surprise turned to sadness for the President. He probably couldn't imagine the horror of little children being bombed, and didn't think it was possible for humans to do this to one another.

In 1986, the government allowed me to study in Cuba, and that is where I met my future husband. My mother didn't want me to get involved with men, telling me I had suffered enough in my life and that I should live in the temple! I didn't think anyone would want me, the way I looked. My husband loved me for my soul—that is real love. We were permitted to go to Moscow after we got married. Our flight had a stop-over in Newfoundland, and I didn't tell him at the time, but my plan was to ask for refugee status in Canada. He agreed, and we were granted asylum by the government. We have lived in Canada and in Ontario ever since.

My mother and father live with us. We feel like we were adopted as family when we moved here. In Ontario, everyone has access to health care, education and social services. My mother says, "Canada is heaven". And I say, "Almost."

For me, war is never necessary. It causes destruction and horror and pain. Little children become victims. We must build communities of love and tolerance. I do wear a poppy on Remembrance Day and I do participate in Remembrance Day ceremonies, because we should never forget the sacrifices made for us. But we should resolve our differences peacefully. It is possible. It starts with healing the heart. Trust in God—it is the best medicine because it is real.

My life is now dedicated to healing children of war. I recently visited burned victims in Uganda. I shared my story and we prayed together. That is true power. If the "girl in the picture" can learn to forgive, anyone can.

Kim Phuc Phan Thi, OOnt was a child during the Vietnam War. She was severely burned in a napalm bombing attack on the village where she lived with her family. Her pain and terror were captured in a photograph taken June 8, 1972 by Associated Press photographer Nick Ut. The photograph went on to win a Pulitzer Prize, and became a defining image of the 20th century. In 1997, she founded *Kim Foundation International*, which supports international organizations providing free medical assistance to children who are victims of war and terrorism. She lives in the Toronto area with her husband and two sons

Pieta

An evocation of the Madonna, an angel of mercy tends to a wounded soldier.

Acrylic and pastel on canvas, 92 x 122 cm

J. L. Granatstein

THE LESSONS OF HISTORY

It is now 115 years since Canada first sent troops overseas to fight. Since the Boer War, we have fought in the Great and Second World Wars; the Korean War; in some warlike Peacekeeping operations as in Cyprus on several occasions; in Somalia; and Former Yugoslavia; peripherally in the first Gulf War; then in Kosovo, and most recently in Afghanistan. More than 115,000 Canadians have died in service. This country has paid its dues again and again.

But what have we learned from our war experience? What lessons can we draw from a century's conflicts, loss, defeats, and victories?

Historians don't really believe that there are lessons in history. Assad is not Hitler. Ahmedinajad was not Mussolini, even if he was a dangerous buffoon. The times are never in sync, the people involved always different, the challenges and opportunities never the same. And yet, some things do stand out when we think about Canadians and war. Let me point to five maxims that might be construed as lessons of history.

The first maxim is that we will always fight someone else's war. Canadians have never been the aggressor, and we will never start a war. We go into battle to be a good, loyal ally. This is not to suggest that Canada's national interests have not been at stake in our wars, only that they have never been decisive factors in our decision to fight, and we have never considered what they are before we go to war. That was certainly true in South Africa, and true again in 1914—the Dominion was a colony with as much say as the Gold Coast in determining British policy. It was true again in 1939, notwithstanding the *Statute of Westminster* of 1931, which made Canada as independent in foreign policy as it was in domestic matters. Canadian loyalty to Britain was our reason for going to war, not fear of Nazi aggression. Canadian interests were not directly at risk until the Fall of France in June 1940 or, more likely yet, the Japanese attack on Pearl Harbour on December 7, 1941. This was also true in Korea and Kosovo; it was true in Afghanistan although Canadian national interests are probably more directly involved in the fight against Islamist terrorism than they were in opposing the Kaiser and Führer in 1914 and 1939. But that is a discussion for another time and place.

Secondly, we will always go to war as part of an alliance, but we will never have much say in shaping alliance strategy. Canada is simply too small a player to get a very loud voice. We had almost no say in the Great War, although Prime Minister Sir Robert Borden used the Canadian Corps' battlefield performance to win more autonomy within the Empire. We had almost no voice in Allied strategy in World War II, although Mackenzie King used the nation's huge war effort to get a role in the Combined Boards that ran the Allies' economic war and to establish Canada's middle power status. We had no say in Korea, none in Kosovo, and none in Afghanistan—except in trying to get other NATO allies to buy into the war and largely failing. The reality is that Canada is a small power, and small powers do not determine the policies of the great. A little realism on the part of our politicians, our media, and our people would be useful in assessing our role and responsibilities.

A third and more contentious point: Canada is unlikely to be united in war. The sharp anti-military attitudes of the present have their resonance all through our history. We have never fought a war where Canadians en masse supported the effort. And in truth, in all our wars, one substantial part of the population—with many honourable exceptions—largely opted out, public opinion in French Canada being sharply against participation. This was attributable to a lack of political leadership, not to character. We need to remember that it was a Québec politician—Louis St Laurent—who brought Canada into NATO, into the Korean War, and to spending seven per cent of GDP on defence because he was unafraid to lead. We have not had a political leader since 1957 who has done so, not one who has been willing to talk national interests to Québec instead of pandering to the *nationalistes*.

Then, preparedness matters. There will be another war. No historian could say otherwise. There has always been war and, barring an extraordinary change in human nature, regrettably there will always be wars. Thus Canadians either pay for their defence with dollars now or with lives later. The lack of realism, the sense that Canada has only values and no national interests to defend, or at least none we think about, has always meant we are unprepared. We all have fire insurance on our homes against the small chance of a fire, but we refuse to have the national insurance policy that a well-equipped, well-trained military provides. Canadians have never been and are not prepared now. And we will pay in lives yet again. If that doesn't prove that there are no lessons in history, what could?

J. L. Granatstein, OC is a Canadian historian who specializes in political and military history. He served in the Canadian Army from 1956 to 1966, and was head of the Canadian War Museum in Ottawa from 1998 to 2001. He was a driving force behind the building of the museum's permanent home, which opened in 2005.

Finally, Canadians do well fighting wars once we set our mind to the task. At Vimy, Passchendaele, and in the Hundred Days; at Ortona, the Gothic Line, in Normandy, and at the Scheldt; at Kapyong and Kandahar, Canadian grit, determination, and military skill shone through. Though the losses were terrible, uncommon courage was the norm.

On November 11 each year, some Canadians stop to remember. They all should because we live in freedom and relative peace thanks to those who put their lives on the line for us. We must remember all the men and women who gave their todays for our tomorrows. All Canadians must never forget.

Dazzle

This method of painting warships to camouflage them against enemy fire was first used in WWI. An unlikely precursor to Art Deco and abstract pattern painting.

Acrylic on canvas, 90 x 304 cm

Portrait of John McCrae

Young doctor from Guelph who wrote the legendary poem
In Flanders Fields, memorized by generations of Canadian students:

We are the Dead. Short days ago
We lived, felt dawn, saw sunset glow,
Loved and were loved, and now we lie,
In Flanders fields.

Acrylic and pastel on canvas, 244 x 121 cm

Sally Goddard

WHAT HAVE WE LEARNED FROM WAR?

I had been relatively untouched by war prior to my daughter's involvement in the Afghanistan mission. The only other military person I knew was my father, a medical doctor and artillery officer in the British Army during the Second World War. He never really talked about his past experiences, but the Afghan War changed all that.

Nichola visited my parents before being deployed, and my father shared stories with her I never knew. He recounted his involvement in the Battle of Monte Cassino, the fear he felt, and how he held it together for his wounded comrades. Locked in a farmhouse basement when a retreat was called, he and the others remained there for two days, while the battle raged above. Eventually, the Allies returned and freed them.

As a young person, Nichola become immersed in Canada's military, and I watched her grow, developing into a confident woman. The Royal Military College initially, then her actual jobs, brought out the best in her. She became articulate and focused. She had always wanted to be in the 1st Regiment of the Royal Canadian Horse Artillery, and she got her wish. Posted to Shilo, Manitoba, her work took her to Roger's Pass, where she and her men used artillery fire to bring down avalanches. She helped fight the huge fires which swept through British Columbia, helicoptering into remote ridges where she and her soldiers descended into the forest.

Then word came that she and her men were to be deployed to Afghanistan. They trained at CFB Wainwright and Suffield in preparation, and completed courses in Gagetown. She was young and relatively inexperienced, but she was recommended for the Forward Observation Officer course, which she passed. I don't know what she would have achieved had she taken a different career path, but her BA (Honours) in English and her fluent bilingualism suggests she would have done well in any field. I do know she loved the military and she loved her men.

In an interview with CTV's Lisa Laflamme, Nichola mentioned not worrying about her own safety, but about how making the wrong decision would affect the safety of "her guys". I think she would have far rather been killed than lose one of "her guys". We hear about the "Band of Brothers" when referring to soldiers and their relationship to each other. It appears that it cuts across generations and gender. In his own way, my father helped prepare Nichola for the realities of war. My father returned annually to his regimental reunions, until the gatherings faded because of the dwindling number of soldiers. I like to think Nichola would have done the same thing, met up with "her guys" annually, checked up on them, discussed their war, and then returned to regular jobs. Those of us, who have not experienced war, we cannot comprehend the camaraderie and the love soldiers feel for each other. And soldiers do not forget.

The Afghan War showed the commitment of Canadian soldiers to the cause. Nichola believed in the mission, believed that Canada was doing the honourable thing. On March 4, 2006, she wrote:

> *The longer we are in theatre and the more we interact with the Afghan people, the more I feel we are serving a purpose here. I think that these people, through the Afghan National Army and the Afghan National Police, are trying to achieve something that we in Canada have long since taken for granted. They lay down their lives daily to try and seize something that is so idealistic it is almost impossible to define. It goes beyond women wearing burkas and children being taught to read and write. The Afghan people have chosen who will lead them.... We are here to assist that legitimate and democratically elected government. It is easy to poke holes in that statement... however, we have to start somewhere. With the best of intentions, we have started in Afghanistan. There is nowhere else I'd rather be right now.*

This belief transcended into action as the war took hold, and Nichola and her men went "outside the wire" countless times to deal with the enemy.

As Canadians, when we think of Afghanistan, we think first of Kandahar province. What we forget is this place is the size of Nova Scotia. In the early days of the war, in 2006, we had about 3500 soldiers in Afghanistan, but only about 650 who patrolled "outside the wire". So, to use the Nova Scotia comparison, one day they were in Truro, the next in Yarmouth, then up to Sydney, then back to Kentville, with short stops in Halifax for a shower, if they happened to be in the area. It was thirty-plus degrees Celsius, they were carrying 100 pounds of kit, and they had no visible enemy. It was a war on many fronts, and one not truly appreciated by those of us at home, even those of us lucky enough to be receiving letters.

Their belief never wavered.

Sally Goddard is an educator and the mother of the late Captain Nichola Goddard (pictured below). Captain Goddard was the first Canadian soldier to call in artillery on an enemy since the Korean War, and on that same day, became the first female Canadian soldier killed in combat. In 2010, Sally and husband Tim Goddard founded the *Nichola Goddard Foundation*, a charitable organization devoted to Nichola's legacy of service, and helping those in need.

I have learned several things about war because of Nichola and my father. I have learned that just because people don't talk about their involvement, it doesn't mean they haven't participated. The sharing of war stories is often private, and the hardships of war brought out the best in both my father and Nichola. The love that soldiers share with each other is a bond that is never broken, in life or in death.

Nichola's memory is honoured through the *Nichola Goddard Foundation*, a charity dedicated to education and health care. Calgary has opened the Captain Nichola Goddard School and the CCGS Captain Goddard M.S.M., a new Canadian Coast Guard Mid-Shore Patrol Vessel, will launch soon. Canada continues to remember Nichola, and we are grateful.

A Cross the Channel

Symbolic depiction of a soldier contemplating his imminent demise, evoking the crucifixion.

SHAKESPEARE:
Cowards die many times before their deaths;
The valiant never taste of death but once.
Of all the wonders that I yet have heard,
It seems to me most strange that men should fear;
Seeing that death, a necessary end,
Will come when it will come.

Acrylic and pastel on canvas, 102 x 67 cm

Lt.-Gen. the Hon. Roméo A. Dallaire (retd)

WHAT HAVE WE LEARNED FROM WAR?

There is no greater abuse of human rights than when the frictions of our differences degenerate into conflict and war. Over the last two decades, as we have seen too many mass atrocities perpetrated upon innocent civilian populations, we have finally created the international instruments to combat lawlessness. The United Nations created courts, such as International Criminal Tribunals, to prosecute those responsible for crimes against humanity. These bodies are the vanguard of justice as we work toward a peaceful world. The obligation of this commitment to human rights will be inherited by the youth of our era, who are the generation without borders and who are the future voice of the NGO community around the world.

This will not be the first time that youth has committed itself with such energy and enthusiasm to a cause of justice, and in so doing, paid in large numbers the ultimate price for the cause. I refer, of course, to the scale of the Canadian participation in the World War I effort overseas.

It was a policy that those recruited to serve in combat should meet the fundamental criterion of being adult males 18 years of age and over. But in the hustle and bustle of a reorganized mobilization plan that Sir Sam Hughes (the Canadian Minister of Militia and Defence during World War I) initiated at the beginning of our engagement, a number of rules were not necessarily followed to the letter. This permitted a certain lax application of the age rule, and as a result, the Canadian contingent found itself manned by a significant number of 16 and 17 year-old (and even the odd 15 year-old) boys. By the time they reached the front, a number of them had been found out, and with great disappointment and *amertume*, they were sent home, with a pat on the back and a thank you from their colleagues who continued their march towards the trenches.

Combat requires the energy, the verve, the willful commitment often without regard for danger that really only youthful persons possess. And so when exposed to the extremes of physical deprivations, to the constant stress of being targeted and indiscriminately destroyed, to facing the danger of being blown to pieces in the accomplishment of a mission that too often in that great war seemed impossible, these young men did not waver. The blood, the guts, the sweat, the tears and the pain that they had to endure every day and night for four years, in the most appalling physical conditions and mental duress, are examples of the stoutness, the resilience and the unbridled commitment that only youth can bring to the fray.

These young Canadians fought with such outstanding bravery that other countries noticed, admiring our new nation for our innovative approach to combat, and the victorious results that battles such as Vimy Ridge provided the Allied forces. The Canadian Expeditionary Force was held in high regard not because of its size, nor the numbers of great generals that led the force, although Sir Arthur Currie was exemplary as a tactical commander in his time, but because of the fervor and the doggedness of the individual Canadian citizen soldier. It was he who, inspired by the fraternity and cohesion found within his units, carried the day, even when a number of his colleagues were left lying on the hard fought ground gained that day.

The engagement of youth in horrific scenarios such as war is a fact of history, a seemingly ongoing story of friction degenerating into conflict between humans. This fact puts enormous pressure on senior leadership to ensure that the troops under their command are used sparingly and effectively, so that the scars of the experience of war do not affect negatively the social fabric of a nation in the post war era, when these young veterans come back so heavily affected by this extreme experience. We were not quite ready to handle the large scale of hundreds of thousands of these war-affected youths making their way back into the civilian life that they had left behind before World War I. A number of them continued to suffer for decades in silence, and that is why the creation of the Royal Canadian Legion, the construction of significant commemoration monuments and the decorum and dignity surrounding Remembrance Day ceremonies on November 11 were so important to them, and ultimately to Canadian society.

There is a saying that "war is hell". No one has been to hell as such, yet what soldiers endure in war, in the destruction of human beings, and the fear and loneliness of combat has got to be the closest we could ever imagine hell to be. Having lived that experience, soldiers become the most ardent advocates of peace.

Lieutenant-General Roméo A. Dallaire, OC, CMM, GOQ, MSC, CD is a Canadian senator, humanitarian, author and retired general. In 1993, He was appointed Force Commander for the United Nations Assistance Mission for Rwanda, where he witnessed the country's descent into chaos and genocide, which led to the deaths of more than 800,000 Rwandans. He is an outspoken advocate for human rights, genocide prevention, mental health and war-affected children. He founded *The Roméo Dallaire Child Soldiers Initiative*, an organization committed to ending the use of child soldiers worldwide.

Trench Letter

A large triptych recalls the barren sweep of the scorched battlefield from the perspective of exhausted soldiers huddled in the crevice of a trench, one of whom writes a letter home. Their helmets suggest halos.

Acrylic and pastel on canvas, 182 x 332

Joseph Boyden

VIMY MEMORIAL

That bit of pasture and bush in northern France cradling Vimy Ridge is as close to a colony as Canada might ever have. Interesting to think about, this reverse migration. 97 years ago, on April 9th, all four divisions of the Canadian Army came together for the first time, 100,000 lice-infested, belligerent, rebellious, and impeccably prepared soldiers, asked to do what both France and England had catastrophically failed to do in previous years: take a near impenetrable fortress that guarded the Douai Plain, a vital cog in Germany's war machine. A literal uphill battle.

April 9th thunders in, just as each new day has for the last twenty, the roar of a massive Canadian artillery barrage on the German positions so loud and long you don't know if you'll ever hear much of anything again. The rumbling shock and thud of exploding shells has loosened your teeth and created a week's long migraine. But this morning is different.

The shaking of the earth is muffled because you are underground, squeezed into a long and dimly lit chalk cavern, one of thousands of stinking men ready to pour out from holes in the dirt when the whistle blows. You're a young buck from Saskatoon. A thirty-year-old father of three from Toronto. A minister from Vancouver. A clerk from Montréal. You've stood in this tunnel for hours with no room to lie or even sit down. Suddenly officers shout. The push of men, the dig of their rifles into your back and you are moving through the tunnel, forced from it like a fish down a stream, climbing the steps to the fresh air and small light above you, rifle clenched in your hands so hard your fingers are numb. Outside, it is snowing.

You've trained for this all winter, just one of 30,000 men who go over the top today, Easter Monday, but the intensity of the explosions all around you, the rattling of machine guns as you climb from your cave and onto open ground, facing mud and craters and strings of barbed wire, all of it laid out on a hill before you that you must climb, all of this incredible noise, turns your mind to a screaming blank. Men near you begin to fall, some dead before they hit the ground, others writhing in pain. But you can't stop to help them. You must push up the hill.

The Canadian artillery officers have timed this attack down to the second, and they send a hail of shells just in front, a creeping barrage that offers you some cover from the

German machinegunners. You and the men in your section walk behind this curtain of flame just quickly enough not to fall behind too far, just slowly enough not to be destroyed by your own artillery.

You, the young man from Saskatoon, you stumble over a dead Canadian in front of you right as a hail of fire knocks down the ones behind you. Crawling back onto your feet again, your only thought is of how lucky you are to have tripped when, that very second, the machinegun opens up again, and you stumble back, trying to make sense of what's just happened. It feels like you've been whacked in the chest by a sledgehammer and now you are on your back, the snow falling onto your face, your ears ringing loud enough to block out the scream of the shells above you. Some of the ones who survived their wounds say they felt nothing, only a numbness when they were hit, but that's not the case for you. You can feel with each heartbeat the blood pump out. You know what's coming, do what you swore to yourself you'd never do. You cry out for your mother, for her embrace. But you won't feel that again.

You, the thirty-year-old from Toronto, a photo of your young family tucked safely in your tunic, you and your section have been given the task of taking an advance German trench, but you've lost the others in the smoke and the noise and the darkness that's just beginning to lighten now. They must be ahead. You've been stumbling slowly up this incline, too slowly it seems. You begin to rush, the fear of losing the others the most frightening thought in the whole world. To be all alone out here makes you want to piss your pants. Your quick walk becomes a run, and you are screaming for your friends, never knowing you rush into your own barrage. A scream from above, but not enough time to recognize your mistake, to realize that you've gotten too far ahead, or to think of your children and your wife tucked safely in bed back home.

You, the minister from Vancouver, your job is simple. Console the wounded and perform last rites for the dying. You huddle in a crater with a group of dead. These ones around you might be sleeping they look so peaceful. No obvious wounds on their bodies, they lie back almost comfortably in the mud. A 5.9 German shell landed close by them as they tried to take cover in this hole, its immense blast concussing their bodies so violently that it turned their internal organs into instant jelly. Nothing for you to do here but bless each one and close some eyes. You climb out of the crater and walk upright like a human again, kneel to a young wounded one and ask him his name, if he wishes to be blessed. You don't know, will never know, that a German sniper on the rise has spotted your movement, and as you raise your hand to the young man's forehead, the crack of the rifle that kills you isn't audible in the scream and roar.

And you, a clerk from Montréal, you and your section are some of the first to sweep into the German line, this confusing, snaking array of deep trenches and tunnels. You are one of the first Allies to stand on this ground, this hill held by the Germans for two-and a-half years. But you're not thinking of that. The hand-to-hand fighting is ferocious, the enemy surprised, wide-eyed like boys to see Canadians screaming and bayoneting and throwing Mills bombs and shooting up and down the alleys that, it is said, could never be taken. You, Montréal clerk, you are part of this snarling animal that the Germans have come to fear, and you take part in it, this killing that happens close enough and with your bare hands gripping a knobkerrie or a trench knife to see the eyes of those who don't look much different than you. You look down the hill you've just climbed and see hundreds of Canadians, thousands coming to your aid. A German sergeant runs bellowing up behind you, smashes your head two-fisted with his club. You feel nothing except for what you think is the brush of your wife's bare foot along your calf.

Droves and droves of us Canadians go over the top this morning. For almost 4000, Easter Monday 1917, is our last day on earth.

Almost ten decades later, nature has allowed us to forget what happened here. Almost. From below it, the ridge is a gentle-seeming rise of hardwood forest and verdant pasture. Sheep graze in and around the concave dips that dot the fields. Thousands of dips—old shell holes and craters filling in slowly with time. Walk with us up this rise that leads to the monument, walk with my friend Jim, my son, and me. We've come to trace Jim's grandfather's steps. We've come to try and teach my teenaged boy how history still lives. How it still breathes.

We stray off the maple-lined road that leads us to our little piece of Canada in France. We are immediately surrounded by new, lime-green forest, some of it growing out of old German support trenches. Moss blankets the ground. Birds call out. Jacob goes off exploring, and when he returns, he carries a piece of human bone, asking what it might be. We place it back where he found it. Look at my son, a blue-eyed teen toying with the idea of joining the military. Lots of dead soldiers his age, always his same age, lie here under our feet.

The walk uphill to the monument looks deceptively easy, but we're all breathing hard. No 70-pound packs on our shoulders today, no heavy rifles in our hands. No mud or dead bodies or barbed wire, no bullets or bombs going off around us.

The highest point of the ridge, Hill 145, holds the monument on its back. Open fields surround it, the earth still pummeled into waves by 90-year-old artillery. Figures carved from limestone, some shrouded in stone veils, circle two huge pillars etched with the names of our missing, our dead. Step up. Walk forward. Lean against the cool limestone. Your two hands just barely cover the names of four dead. Four lives imprinted on your palms.

That clerk from Montréal, he is the kid at the café who serves you coffee each morning. That minister from Vancouver, he's the one you had over for dinner last Sunday who asked for seconds of the roast. That thirty-year-old from Toronto, he's your co-worker who keeps the pictures of his family on his desk. That young one from Saskatoon, he's my son.

The Douai Plain stretches out beyond the monument. Listen now, carefully, as Jim explains: The Allied High Command didn't expect the Canadians to take this ridge that day. Our action was simply a ruse for other major assaults to the south. But we took it. And there was no backup plan in the case of victory, so all we could do was hold our ground and watch the Germans run.

We continue to stare. Jim points down the plain. "That path there leads straight to Germany."

"A waste, then," I say.

"No, not a waste," Jim says, scanning the same ground his grandfather walked. He bends to pick up a small stone as Jacob lopes towards the monument. I watch my son, his shape a contemporary sag of baggy clothes and lank blond hair, and he is so beautiful my breath catches in my chest. Jim is right. Jim is so very right.

Joseph Boyden is a Canadian novelist and short story writer. His first novel, *Three Day Road,* won the Amazon/*Books in Canada* First Novel Award and the Rogers Writers' Trust Fiction Prize. His second novel, *Through Black Spruce*, won the 2008 Scotiabank Giller Prize, and his third book, *The Orenda,* was named the winner of the 2014 edition of Canada Reads. Of Irish, Scottish and Anishinaabe heritage, Boyden writes about First Nations heritage and culture. Boyden's father, Raymond Wilfrid Boyden, was a medical officer renowned for his bravery, awarded the Distinguished Service Order, and was a highly decorated medical officer in World War II.

Cortège

A group of war-weary exhausted soldiers returning to barracks after a gas attack.

Acrylic on canvas, 152 x 213 cm

Prof. Margaret MacMillan

WHY SHOULD WE REMEMBER THE FIRST WORLD WAR?

We often prefer not to think about war, to see it as an aberration and interruption of the normal, and peaceful, state of affairs. War, however, is deeply woven into human history. A century ago, the Great War broke out in Europe and in the course of the next four years drew in over twenty world nations, including, of course, our own. The impact and consequences of that gigantic struggle were huge, and we cannot understand the 20th century without taking that into account.

As Canadians commemorate what is now called the First World War, we should reflect that many others, from India to Serbia, are remembering it too. The war, which few had expected would last for over four years, destroyed lives: nine million soldiers died and many more were wounded, women lost husbands or those they might have married, and children grew up fatherless.

The rich and prosperous continent of Europe, which had dominated the world before 1914, wasted the lives of its peoples and poured out its resources in the war. It has never recovered its former strength and position. Moreover, without the strains imposed by the war, old regimes might not have totally collapsed. Russia was already changing fast, but the war finished off Tsarism and made possible the Communists' seizure of power, with long term consequences both for Russians themselves, and the world. Austria-Hungary and the Ottoman Empire fell to pieces and in their place new and often shaky states appeared. Too often these new countries were based on a single ethnicity which marginalized minorities, whether Shia in Iraq or Germans in Czechoslovakia. Worse still, the war brutalized European society and helped pave the way for the rise of extremist movements of both the right and the left. It did not bring a lasting peace, but rather created the conditions which eventually led to the Second World War in 1939.

For other countries though, the war prompted more welcome changes. The United States, which entered on the Allied side in 1917, moved closer to becoming a superpower. In the great European empires, independence movements grew stronger. Canada, like Australia, New Zealand, Newfoundland and South Africa, already had a measure of self-government. The war, though, and the realization that Canada played a major role in contributing soldiers, goods, raw materials and money, speeded this country's growing maturity. At the start of the First World War our prime minister, Sir Robert

Borden, deferred to British leadership. By its third year he was banging on the table and demanding a change in the war's management. At the subsequent peace conference in Paris, Canada insisted on being present as a full member, signing the treaties and joining the League of Nations in its own right.

In the 21st century, we have yet another reason for looking back at the First World War. Our world, in several key ways, resembles that of 1914. We are seeing shifts in the international order, with some powers rising and others declining.

The United States may be in the same position the British Empire was then—as a hegemony which has dominated the world and much of its trade, now challenged by new and often brash powers. In 1914, it was Germany, Russia and the United States emerging as heirs to British supremacy. Today, it is China, India or Brazil asserting its strength against the mighty United States.

We, too, have seen a series of crises which have weakened the international order, and are conscious of the world's trouble spots, where local tensions or rivalries have the potential to drag in larger powers. A hundred years ago the Balkans were dangerous; today it is Syria, Ukraine and the South China Sea. Why, in 1914, did tensions go over the edge into all-out war? It was a mystery at the time, and has been ever since. And that is worrying. If we don't understand how the First World War happened, we might also find ourselves accidentally in a war.

In 1914, many people assumed that the spread of trade and investment had linked nations so closely together that they would not rationally chose war: the costs for everyone would be too high. We, too, live in an age of globalization which is binding the world together economically, and through rapid communications and mass movements of peoples. We assume that this closeness can only have harmonious benefits. Yet that other great period of globalization in modern times should give us second thoughts. Before the First World War, the reaction to globalization heightened nationalism, and spurred imperial rivalries. So we should be careful of complacency.

Great disasters can also bring recognition that changes must come, and that was certainly true in 1919. The American president, Woodrow Wilson, articulated for many war-weary Europeans their hopes of a better, fairer and more peaceful world.

Margaret MacMillan, OC is a professor of history at the University of Toronto and is currently at the University of Oxford, where she is a professor of international history, and warden of St Antony's College. She is a former provost of Trinity College at the University of Toronto and was previously at Ryerson University. A leading expert on history and international relations, MacMillan is a frequent commentator in the media. She is the author or editor of ten books, most recently, *The War That Ended Peace: How Europe Abandoned Peace for the First World War.*

In his scheme for a League of Nations to provide collective security, a new diplomacy, and self-determination of peoples, he drew on ideas which had been well-discussed in Europe for decades. We tend to judge the League too harshly, because it did not prevent another global war. But we should remember what it did achieve, whether in settling disputes between nations, promoting disarmament, or furthering human well-being through entities such as the International Labour Organization. Ultimately, the League introduced the idea that it was possible to develop and manage an international order, and that the world was not condemned to anarchy in which nations jostled for advantage. That idea, and that hope, never went away. Even during the Second World War, Allied statesmen were planning a successor to the League, and for new international economic institutions. This time, under the wise leadership of President Franklin Roosevelt, the United States became a leader in building the new order, and itself joined the new institutions, such the United Nations and the World Bank.

Today, we are still trying to build a strong international order, to keep as many states as possible within international society. That endeavour must not end.

Airborne

A fragile war plane defies gravity. This was the first war to use airplanes to bomb enemy targets.

Acrylic and pastel on canvas, 198 x 122 cm

Mellissa Fung

WHAT HAVE WE LEARNED FROM WAR?

In the fall of 2008, during the height of Canada's military involvement in Afghanistan, I travelled to Kabul to tell a war story; a story of anxious mothers, fathers and children fleeing their villages because they no longer felt safe. It had been a terrible summer of fighting in the southern provinces, in Kandahar, Helmand, and Uruzgan, and in their desperation to escape, thousands of families packed up their possessions and headed north.

Many ended their journey at the Charahi Qambar refugee camp on the outskirts of Kabul, a sprawling, tacked-together jumble of tents, shacks and anything else that offered shelter. There was the barefooted shoemaker from Kandahar who made me tea in his mud hut; a mother who was left with just two of her five children, having lost the others and her husband in a bombing; the distraught camp elder who told me he was going to have to start turning people away. In all their stories, the trauma was reflected in the dark circles under their eyes and the weary rasp of their voices. I was a sympathetic witness to their misery, and though I didn't know it then, I would soon be a casualty of the same war.

I've replayed the moment a million times: a blue car, three men jumping out with AK-47s pointed at our heads; my fixer forced to the ground and begging for his life. A knife slicing into my shoulder, and then into my left hand as I fought back. Shoved into the back seat, bloody and frightened; my face hard against the dirty floor. Feet on my head and on my back. The car speeding away, and after an hour, stopping at the foot of a mountain. Forced out of the car at gunpoint. And then we hiked, hiked for hours, arriving at a town I would later come to know was Maidan, in Wardak province. As darkness fell that night, they threw me into an even darker place—a hole in the ground. It led to a tunnel, about 10 feet down, and that led to a slightly larger hole. I could barely stand up in it.

That was my home for the next 28 days. It's where I would wait for my scabs to fall off. Where I was essentially starved, fed a diet of juice pouches and sickly-sweet crème-filled cookies. And it's where I was violently assaulted at knifepoint on one of my first nights as a hostage.

But it was also the place where I got to know Khalid. I'm sure that's not his real name, but he was the one kidnapper who showed me some kindness. We spent days and nights in that hole together, sharing cigarettes, learning each other's language. He told me about his girlfriend, Shagufa. He had stolen my camera on that first day, but he started bringing it back to show me pictures he had taken of her. There was Shagufa on the screen of my camera, giggling at him. There she was with her sisters and her mother. He promised me he wouldn't kill me, and I trusted him. Sometimes he brought me rice and bread. Twice he brought me French fries, which he said Shagufa made.

We talked about the war. About women. He did not believe Shagufa should go to school. Or get a job. He wanted to be a suicide bomber and he wanted Shagufa to follow him in a martyr's death. On our last night together, as he led me blindfolded down the mountain—to be freed in a prisoner exchange negotiated by the Afghan government—he asked me for forgiveness.

"Do not hate me, Mellissa," he said. I assured him I did not, because I saw in him the lost potential of a generation of young Afghans. Desperate, orphaned perhaps, driven by ignorance and ideology, the same motives that drive conflict everywhere else in the world. He suffered, so I suffered.

In that hole, I learned that even in the horrible midst of war, when all hope seems lost, there can be understanding, kindness, and forgiveness. My education would continue when I came home and spent months interviewing soldiers coping with crippled bodies and tortured minds. The courageous Billy Kerr, a corporal who lost both legs and an arm. Captain Trevor Greene, whose skull was split open by an axe attack leaving him unable to walk or speak. Medic Kevin Moore who kept flashing back to the day his friend Chad O'Quinn was killed in an IED attack. Some returned with wounds to the body, some with wounds to the soul.

The worst losses were those suffered by the families whose sons and daughters, mothers and fathers, never came home. Canada sacrificed 158 soldiers, a diplomat, two aid workers, and a journalist to war in the Afghan desert. In their stories, I learned about the courage to continue, and about the depth of forgiveness. Witness Reine Dawe, whose 26-year-old son Matthew was killed in 2007: "Somebody asked me, do you hate the young men who killed Matt? And I said of course not. I don't know who he was, but he was a young guy doing what he thought was the right thing to do. And he has a mother; he has a family, and he's a victim of his circumstances just as Matt was."

Reine now works with a Canadian NGO bringing education to Afghan children in the belief that it will create opportunities for young girls and boys, like my kidnapper Khalid; like the young man who planted the bomb who killed her son. That is how she copes; that is what she has learned.

War changes lives—forever, in ways visible and invisible. Nothing is absolute in war, not even death. I have learned that some scars never fully heal, not for me, not for any of the soldiers and their families. But it is in our determination not to surrender to war's darkest moments that we find the clarity of understanding and the will to forgive.

Journalist and former CBC correspondent Mellissa Fung has been on the frontlines covering a wide range of stories on both Canadian and world affairs for the last 20 years. Her first book, *Under an Afghan Sky*, chronicles her experience as a hostage after she was kidnapped while on assignment in Afghanistan in 2008. Fung lives in Washington, DC.

The Painted Flag

Although not created until 50 years after this war, the new maple leaf flag has come to symbolize Canadian nationhood with eloquence. Here it suggests half-mast as a mark of respect for those who made the ultimate sacrifice.

Acrylic on canvas, 131 x 101 cm

The Rt. Hon. Jean Chrétien

WHAT HAVE WE LEARNED FROM WAR?

When I was young, war was a part of my life and the life of my family.

When Prime Minister Mackenzie King was elected during the World War II era, he had promised that there would be no conscription. However, as the seriousness of the war developed, he changed his mind and held a plebiscite. Quebecers had all voted for King, and by that time France had collapsed and made peace with the Germans, so the real danger was in Great Britain.

The referendum results came as no surprise—over 75 per cent of Francophones voted against conscription. My father, however, voted yes. He felt that because Canada had declared war against Germany, it was our duty as citizens to fight for our country. In the villages around Québec, my father's view represented a small minority. The result of the plebiscite created tension between neighbours.

The tradition at that time was to put a flag in the window when someone in a home was serving in the military. We were the only family in our group of row houses to have a flag on display. Although my father voted for conscription, there was no question any of his sons would be conscripted. He felt strongly that they should volunteer, and that is what three of my brothers did.

My sister's fiancé also enlisted, and was stationed in London, England. As with many loved ones, she waited anxiously for letters from him. One of my family chores was to go pick up the mail. One day I wanted to tease her, so I hid all of her fiancé's letters from her. She wanted to throttle me! Our family would send him care packages of candy, *sucre à la crème*, and occasionally sneak him a bottle of Canadian whisky. We were all part of the war effort, and we were proud of that.

It is never easy to convince people to go to war, and it is rare that people will vote for it. But sometimes war is necessary.

When the United States was attacked by terrorists on September 2001, I was one of the first foreign leaders to make the decision to use Article 5 of the NATO charter. Under the charter it states that if one member of NATO is attacked, we are all obligated to respond. The attack had originated in Afghanistan, so we decided collectively, and with the support of the United Nations, to go to war in Afghanistan.

As Prime Minister, you worry about the troops when you decide to send them into conflict zones, and into harm's way.

It weighs heavily on you, and you reflect on it when you are alone, far away from the cameras and Parliament.

When soldiers or civilians were killed, I would quietly pray for them. At times of war, a Prime Minister makes decisions for the good of the nation, and soldiers know that when they sign up to serve, they may go to war, and they may die.

One thing you do not worry about is how your decision makes you look as Prime Minister. It is all about what is right and what is wrong, and if you waiver, you can make a lot of mistakes.

I was very skeptical about the claim that Iraq had weapons of mass destruction. I told US President George W. Bush that if he did not have the support of the UN, Canada would not be going to war. We were briefed on almost the same information as the Americans, but I did not see any proof. A year before the US invaded Iraq, I told Mr. Bush that we wouldn't go if they didn't meet the conditions. In the end, the UN did not sanction the invasion of Iraq, so we did not go.

Deciding to go to war, or not go to war, has its consequences. If you lose the next election, so be it. When deciding whether or not to participate in the Iraq War, I had to take into consideration our economic ties with the US. Business people put pressure on me, saying the US would retaliate and stop buying from us if we didn't join them. I asked them to "give me a list of all the goods and services the Americans are buying from us and they don't need". I am still waiting for that list. Business is business. People buy what they need.

Yes, it caused a lot of problems for some people, but now we can clearly see that my Government made the right decision.

I hope for future generations that we never see war on the scale of what we saw in the First and Second World Wars. War today in the 21st century stems often from ethnic, religious and regional tensions, which leads to borderless terrorism rather than traditional country vs. country warfare. Also, the tools of war today are technologically more advanced: drones, satellites, and the threat of global nuclear war.

The Right Honourable Jean Chrétien, PC, OM, CC, QC was Prime Minister of Canada from November 4, 1993 to December 12, 2003. He was first elected to the House of Commons in 1963, and was re-elected 11 times. He served in many ministerial positions and won three majority governments. Mr. Chrétien was Prime Minister during the wars in Afghanistan and Iraq.

So what have we learned from war? Not to have more wars. When people are educated and live well, they tend to be content. The recipe for unrest and violence is often rooted in poverty, misery, famine, the lack of basic health services and education. Therefore, we, as communities and countries, must take care of one another.

We have also learned that in order to deal with religious fanaticism, we need to have more inter-faith dialogue, not less.

In the end, we all worship the same creative force. Happiness and peace for everyone is something we all strive to achieve. As Prime Minister, I dedicated myself to this goal for the people of Canada at home and abroad.